In From Arm's Length

Christina Rombouts

BookLeaf Publishing

India | USA | UK

Presentation by *BookLeaf Publishing*

Web: www.bookleafpub.com

E-mail: info@bookleafpub.com

ISBN:9789358316520

First edition 2024

DEDICATION

To every person in my tapestry, and to the God
who weaved it: thank you.

Nocturne

My thoughts swim far above me
Trying to reach the top
Trying to break the surface tension
Trying to reach my God.

Sealed tight, I feel,
In hollowed out distraction
Caught fast in things I wish I didn't feel
Were worth my wasted passion.

Like stones, they hold me low
And keep me far from you
I'm bound by pangs of want and dread
And words of thanks unused.

What's there for me to do?
What's the link – the bridge to you?
Where am I supposed to be tonight?
What am I not doing right?

I'm here; you're there, not here
I speak; I don't know what I hear
Is that my own wish echoed back?
Is there some way to know that I'm not going
mad?

What Did You Say?

The older words you said
I sifted,
And clung to the lightest of them.
Tucked them beneath my sleeping head at night
Pressed them into a favorite book,
Like a daisy.
Now, you gave me new words.
They are rolling marbles in my skull
From right to left,
Front to back.
The sad words are stickier –
I try to pull them from my fingertips.
What if there are no good words this time?
Someday I will learn to close my hands around
what I have
And close my lips around my open mouth.

Don't Get Your Feelings Hurt

A reel of stills tells our story
There are pieces missing
Bits clipped out when we sealed our mouths
They resume.
The pictures prick my brain
In the middle of a meal; a sentence
A lane-change
An apology
A key-turn.
I'm in your front seat
Your kitchen
Soothing the white cracks on your knuckles.
Pressing my cheek to your sleeping back.
They clip past,
Momentary.

Spring

You remind me of spring.
It was spring when I sat at my desk
Waiting for three drawn-out knocks to send my
gut to my throat.
Spring nights, I couldn't help but look for you.
It was those early days of spring when my
questions multiplied each time we spoke.
We seemed so close,
Yet I couldn't ask the one thing I needed to.
Cool March air through an open window feels
like you.
Spring was when things were fresh and
undecided,
Though the clues had been there since autumn.
That spring, you told me I was your best friend –
That I was the girl-version of you.
I valued nothing more than being the object of
your fascination.
I let my imagination do funny things that spring,
But I never thought I'd see you follow.
Late in May, it was pried from you that you
would marry soon.
My gut never left my throat.
I felt betrayed by you both,
Though I had no right.

I sat absorbing the happy details,
Stunned like a child who is struck for being
childish.
You can hardly blame the thing.
That was the last day of spring.

I Knew You

Do you believe
that the same fingers that dusted each shore
with black and white sand,
that laid gossamer wings into the dragonfly's
spine,
that carved the faces of snow-capped Alps,
and hung planets in the sky lifetimes away
knit you, too?

Before You Forget About Me

I wanted to fit a space in you
Previously unknown.
Discover windows with a view
To share with you alone.

Am I young for my advancing age,
Or have you been burned by time?
Has no one ever stirred in you
A feeling so sublime?

I'll learn every line of you
Commit your soul to memory
No living being will know you better
Apart from Him who wrote your melody.

Struck blind and deaf at once, my love
Even then I'd know your presence
The immortal bridge between us two
Is love's distilled quintessence.

I've long since swept my mind, dear one
Of any one before you
Aired out and emptied all except for
Every feature that adorns you.

If it's not too much to ask of you
The one thing that I'll need
Is only that you lose your mind
Before you forget about me.

I Hesitate

My mind swells with
Every path I didn't take.
Every yes I didn't say
Evaporates.

The crushing weight
of leaps of faith
will bury me
while I hesitate.

Your Name

Your name is like a needle;
I recoil.
It has lived so many lives in mine,
But I never had that effect on you.
For me, you erupted in a hot, beautiful flame –
Now extinguished.
For you, I glided towards the sky,
Then turned to land safely on the ground.

Torrential Love

Who were you before the lines grew
Deeper on your olive cheeks?
You were a man shrouded in impeccable logic;
A fortress of measured emotion.
But years of trickling warmth,
Bad jokes,
Kisses on your palms,
And torrential love
Running over
Softened the scab on your heart.
I'd never want a different brand of love than
yours.

Your Sea

I never made
A single wave
In your sea.

Fitful Sleep

Night thoughts aren't your real thoughts.
They're just the concentrated exhaust
Of your daytime thoughts.
Squeeze tightly all the thoughts of your day,
And the sticky balm on your hands –
The residue –
Can't hurt you.

Visiting Hours

In hospital sunlight,
Dirty windows cast hazy streaks
And make her husband's glasses shine
While he sets his watch.
He watches her breathe
In rhythm with the neon lines.
They both slow.
The light is lower now.
Dinner comes and sits untouched.
Morning coffee jells in Styrofoam cups.
Her skin glows less today,
But he doesn't want to notice.
Visiting hours are ending now,
Except in special circumstances.
A voice overhead pages Doctor So-and-So.
He scoots forward now to link their hands.
He thinks of the first, the middle
And the last of their Saturday dances.
This many years should have felt like longer,
no?
His crackling voice floats familiar words to her
ear.
She was supposed to follow.
Her eyelids flicker,
But they tell him it might not mean anything.

She was everything.
He'd rather go with her.

Your Admirer

I loved you faster
From a house of glass
Exposed my every notion

You stained my mind
Like the highest tide
Before retreating to the ocean

What casts light on your darkest corners?
I thought I might decode it
I loved so much your shadowy heart
When you hardly even showed it

I tug the thread that lines your head
And study all the knots
I'd hoped by now I'd understand
The arrangement of your thoughts

If I never turn into the girl
Who captures your attention
You'll be deeply loved for all time
And I'll have learned my lesson.

Together

I hold the hand
of every man
who ever loved me well.
We walk together
toward the girl
who's going to save him now.

The Stream

You were my nameless crisis; it had no face but
yours.
I searched within for what was killing me,
But it was the stream I drank with you.

Languishing

My vaporizing thoughts
Float from mind to ceiling
And condense once more at daybreak's light
For a day full of re-feeling.

In From Arm's Length

I ache with the absence of you.
I crave the calm
The shadows
Your veiled expressions
Your strength.
Would they be less potent if I had you purely?
If you brought me in from arm's length?

Come Home

I want to breathe in again
the warm earth from your chest,
Feel the softness of your sleeping breath on my
head.
"Tell me a joke before we turn off the light"
Tell me we're inseparable;
That everything's all right.
I'm starting to lose that thing that you do
When you begin a laugh.
I'd picked it up, but not on purpose
Now it's fading in the black.

Doubt's Benefit

If I could give you such a gift
So as to understand my plight
To convey a tiny fraction of
My inmost being's fight

Might you begin forgiving
My lapse of perfect tact?
Forget the times I say the words
Then try to take them back?

I grew my soul in certain soil
That your hands have never felt
I'm made of parts you'll never grasp
But I know that can't be helped.

Across this ample chasm
Where all my rotten words fell
I ask for grace extended
While I try to love you well.

Cosmos

Darkness hangs
Between stars without names
And edges of galaxies
No human eye will see.
A light is extinguished
A lightyear away
And I am still in the same square foot.
Next to you, I condense
To take up a little less room.

My Frozen Mouth

I strung words together, once again
And offered them to you.
I tried explaining,
A little better this time,
but they echo just the same.
Sounds don't exist
In my frozen mouth
That well enough describe the
vicious conflict draped around me.

www.ingramcontent.com/pod-product-compliance
Lightning Source LLC
La Vergne TN
LVHW050248200726
843509LV00015B/2938